LANZAROTE Travel Guide 2024

Whispers of Timanfaya Lanzarote's Secrets Unwrapped - From Lava Fields to Moonlit Craters

CHERYL JOHN

Table of Contents

Introduction

Nestled amidst the vast embrace of the Atlantic, where the azure waves whisper tales of mystery, lies an island

 that beckons the curious traveler. Picture this: an otherworldly canvas painted with volcanic hues, a tapestry woven by nature's hand. Welcome to Lanzarote, where the ordinary meets the extraordinary, and every step is a dance with wonder.

As the sun dips below the horizon, casting shadows upon the rugged landscape, Lanzarote emerges as an enigma waiting to be unraveled. Imagine standing on the edge of a lunar landscape, where the earth beneath your feet pulses with the echoes of ancient volcanoes. You find yourself asking, "How did this masterpiece of geology come to be?" It's a question that lingers in the air, drawing you deeper into the narrative of this captivating island.

Join me on a journey beyond the tourist brochures, where each page unfolds a story of resilience, innovation, and a touch of the surreal. Lanzarote, with its lunar valleys and surreal vineyards, is not just a destination it's an odyssey through time and nature's creative brilliance.

But wait, there's more. Have you ever wondered what secrets the locals whisper to the wind as the night unfolds? What stories do the stars tell above the quiet beaches and lively plazas? Lanzarote after dark is a chapter of intrigue, where the island's heartbeat quickens, and the adventure takes on a new rhythm.

So, why should you embark on this odyssey? Because Lanzarote is not just a place; it's an immersive experience waiting to be embraced. This guide is not merely a collection of facts; it's a key to unlock the doors of discovery, where every turn of the page reveals a new facet of this captivating island.

Are you ready to trade the ordinary for the extraordinary? Can you feel the magnetic pull of Lanzarote's allure? The journey begins here, where the mundane transforms into the extraordinary, and the familiar becomes the extraordinary. Adventure awaits, dear reader. Let's dive into the pages of "Lanzarote Unveiled: A Journey Beyond the Horizon." Your odyssey starts now.

Destination Overview

Unveiling Lanzarote's Charms

Welcome to the magical world of Lanzarote! Picture  this: pristine beaches, rugged landscapes, and a vibe that's as laid-back as it gets. If you're on the lookout for your next unforgettable getaway, Lanzarote is where it's at.

Let's kick things off with the beaches. Think golden sands meeting crystal-clear waters – it's the stuff postcards are made of. Whether you're a sun-soaker or a water sports enthusiast, Lanzarote's beaches have got you covered. Grab your sunscreen, lay out that beach towel, and let the sound of the waves whisk you away to relaxation paradise.

Now, let's talk about the landscapes. Lanzarote is a feast for the eyes, with its otherworldly volcanic terrain. Timanfaya National Park is a must-see, where you'll feel like you've landed on Mars. The unique rock formations and lava fields create a surreal backdrop that's begging to be explored. Don't forget your camera – you'll want to capture these moments.

Feeling a bit adventurous? How about a trip to Jameos del Agua? This underground cave system turned cultural and recreational space is a hidden gem. Picture yourself strolling through illuminated tunnels and discovering a subterranean lake. It's a one-of-a-kind experience that's bound to leave you in awe.

Now, let's talk flavors. Lanzarote's culinary scene is a delightful fusion of fresh seafood, local produce, and Canarian specialties. Whether you're a foodie or just someone who appreciates a good meal, you'll find yourself savoring every bite. From traditional tapas to seafood paella, the island's restaurants are a treat for your taste buds.

But it's not just about the sights and flavors – Lanzarote has a vibrant culture that's worth exploring. Head to the capital, Arrecife, and wander through the charming streets. You'll stumble upon local markets, boutique shops, and maybe even catch a glimpse of the lively festivals that take place throughout the year.

Now, let's address the practicalities. Getting around Lanzarote is a breeze, thanks to a well-connected network of roads. Renting a car is a popular choice, allowing you the freedom to explore the island at your own pace. And when it comes to accommodations, Lanzarote offers a range of options – from cozy boutique hotels to beachfront resorts.

But here's the kicker – Lanzarote's charm lies not just in its attractions but in the feeling you get when you're there. It's a blend of relaxation, adventure, and a touch of the exotic that sets it apart from your average holiday destination.

So, what are you waiting for? Pack your bags, book that ticket, and get ready to uncover the enchanting charms of Lanzarote. Your next great adventure awaits, and it's calling your name from the shores of this Canary Island paradise.

Getting There

Your Gateway to Paradise

Welcome to your ticket to paradise – Lanzarote! If you're dreaming of an escape to sun-soaked beaches and  breathtaking landscapes, you're in for a treat. Let's dive into how you can make your way to this hidden gem in the Atlantic.

First things first – getting to Lanzarote is a breeze. Hop on a direct flight, and in no time, you'll be touching down on this island of wonders. With several major airlines offering routes to Lanzarote, finding a convenient and affordable option is a piece of cake.

Touching down at Lanzarote Airport, you'll instantly feel the island's warm embrace. The airport is well-equipped, making your arrival smooth and stress-free. Grab your bags, and you're ready to kick off your Lanzarote adventure.

Now, let's talk transportation. While taxis are readily available at the airport, many travelers opt for the freedom of renting a car. It's the ideal way to explore the nooks and crannies of Lanzarote at your own pace. Plus, the roads are well-maintained, making it a joy to navigate the island.

If you're not into driving, fear not Lanzarote's public transportation has got you covered. Buses operate regularly, linking key destinations across the island. It's a convenient and budget-friendly option for those looking to soak in the scenery without worrying about driving directions.

As for accommodations, Lanzarote offers a range of choices to suit every taste and budget. Whether you fancy a beachfront resort, a cozy guesthouse, or a chic boutique hotel, the island has you covered. Booking in advance is a smart move, ensuring you snag the perfect spot for your stay.

Now, let's talk about the main event – the beaches. Lanzarote boasts some of the most stunning beaches in the world. Imagine powdery sands, clear turquoise waters, and a gentle breeze – it's a beach lover's paradise. From Playa Blanca to Famara Beach, each stretch of coastline has its unique charm waiting to be discovered.

But Lanzarote is not just about beaches – the island's volcanic landscapes are a sight to behold. Timanfaya

National Park is a must-visit, offering a surreal experience as you wander through craters and lava fields. It's like stepping onto another planet, and your Instagram followers will thank you for the envy-inducing photos.

As you plan your getaway to Lanzarote, keep in mind the vibrant local culture. Explore the charming streets of Arrecife, try some local Canarian cuisine, and maybe even catch a traditional festival. It's these authentic touches that make your Lanzarote escape truly unforgettable.

In a nutshell, Lanzarote is more than just a destination – it's an invitation to unwind, explore, and create memories that last a lifetime. So, what are you waiting for? Your gateway to paradise awaits, and the adventure of a lifetime is just a flight away. Get ready to discover the magic of Lanzarote – your slice of heaven on Earth..

FAQs

Everything You Need to Know

Welcome to the ultimate guide – your FAQs on all things essential! If you're curious about the ins and outs of a topic, you're in the right place. Let's dive into the questions you've been itching to ask.

Q: What's the best time to visit Lanzarote?
A: Lanzarote boasts a sunny climate year-round, but for the prime beach weather, aim for spring and fall. That's when the temperatures are just right, and you can soak up the sun without feeling like a roasted marshmallow.

Q: How do I get to Lanzarote?
A: Getting to this slice of paradise is a breeze. Several major airlines offer direct flights, making it a convenient hop from various locations. Touch down at Lanzarote Airport, and you're officially in vacation mode.

Q: Is renting a car necessary?
A: While not mandatory, renting a car gives you the freedom to explore the island at your own pace. The roads are well-maintained, and the scenery is too good to rush through. If driving isn't your jam, public buses are a solid alternative.

Q: What are the must-visit beaches?

A: Lanzarote's beaches are the stuff of dreams. Playa Blanca and Famara Beach are fan favorites, offering golden sands and turquoise waters. Each beach has its unique vibe, so explore a few to find your perfect spot in the sun.

Q: Are there budget-friendly accommodations?

A: Absolutely! Lanzarote caters to all budgets. Whether you're into beachfront resorts or charming guesthouses, you'll find options that won't break the bank. Booking in advance ensures you snag the best deals.

Q: What's the deal with Lanzarote's volcanic landscapes?

A: Prepare to be amazed. Timanfaya National Park is a must-see, showcasing the island's volcanic beauty. Wander through the otherworldly terrain, snap some jaw-dropping photos, and revel in the unique experience.

Q: How's the local cuisine?

A: Delightful! Canarian cuisine is a treat for your taste buds. From fresh seafood to traditional tapas, Lanzarote's restaurants serve up a culinary adventure. Don't leave without trying the local specialties – your stomach will thank you.

Q: Is public transportation reliable?

A: Indeed! Buses crisscross the island, making it easy to explore without the hassle of driving. It's a budget-friendly option that lets you enjoy the scenery without worrying about parking.

Q: Any cultural highlights?

A: Dive into the local culture in Arrecife. Wander through charming streets, explore markets, and maybe catch a traditional festival. It's these authentic touches that add a special flavor to your Lanzarote adventure.

Q: What's the overall vibe of Lanzarote?

A: Lanzarote is a perfect blend of relaxation and adventure. Whether you're lazing on the beach, exploring volcanic landscapes, or savoring local flavors, the island has a laid-back charm that'll make your getaway truly unforgettable.

Armed with these FAQs, you're ready to tackle Lanzarote like a pro. So, what are you waiting for? Your island escape awaits, and the answers to your burning questions are just a flight away. Get ready to uncover the magic of Lanzarote!

Fun Facts about Lanzarote

Discover the Hidden Stories

Welcome to the intriguing world of Lanzarote, where every corner has a tale to tell. Buckle up for a journey

into the hidden stories that make this Canary Island a treasure trove of fun facts.

Let's start with the unique landscapes did you know that Lanzarote is home to some seriously surreal scenery? Thanks to its volcanic origins, the island's Timanfaya National Park looks like a movie set for an otherworldly adventure. Picture this: craters, lava fields, and a landscape that feels straight out of a sci-fi flick.

Now, here's a quirky fact Lanzarote's famous architect, César Manrique, left his mark all over the island. He believed in harmonizing art with nature, and you can see his influence in places like Jameos del Agua, a cave-turned-cultural space. It's a cool blend of creativity and the island's natural beauty.

Speaking of creativity, did you know that Lanzarote has its own green superhero? Meet the "Lanzarote Palm," a resilient palm tree that can survive in harsh conditions. It's like the Chuck Norris of the plant kingdom, standing tall against the island's arid climate.

Now, let's talk about the wine. Lanzarote's vineyards have a trick up their sleeves they grow their grapes in little craters protected from the winds by semi-circular walls. It's not just clever, it's a stunning sight to behold, and the wine produced here has a unique flavor thanks to this special cultivation method.

Here's a little nugget for beach enthusiasts Playa de Papagayo isn't just your typical sandy haven. Legend has it that it was a pirate's secret hideout back in the day. Now, it's a picture-perfect beach with a dash of swashbuckling history.

Ever heard of a volcanic grill? Well, in Lanzarote, they've turned up the heat on cooking. At El Diablo Restaurant in Timanfaya National Park, they use the Earth's natural heat from the volcano to grill your food. It's like having a barbecue with Mother Nature as the chef.

And did you know that Lanzarote has its own mini Grand Canyon? Yep, it's called La Geria, and it's a breathtaking valley filled with vineyards. The views are jaw-dropping, and the wine-tasting opportunities are plentiful. Who knew a canyon could be so delightful?

As you explore Lanzarote, keep an eye out for the "Fellows of the Canary Islands." These quirky rock formations are scattered around the island, and locals say they resemble people looking out to sea. It's like Mother Nature's way of playing hide and seek with sculptures.

In a nutshell, Lanzarote is not just a destination it's a treasure chest of hidden stories waiting to be uncovered. From the surreal landscapes to the tales of pirates and palm trees, every moment on this island is a chance to discover something new. So, pack your curiosity and get ready to unravel the hidden stories of Lanzarote – where every fact is stranger than fiction.

Accommodation

Finding Your Home Away.Welcome to Lanzarote where your home away from home awaits! Let's dive into the

nitty-gritty of finding the perfect spot to kick back, relax, and soak in all the island vibes.

Lanzarote is like a hospitality buffet, offering a range of accommodations to suit every taste and budget. Whether you're the type to splurge on a beachfront resort or cozy up in a budget-friendly guesthouse, this island's got you covered.

For those seeking the royal treatment, beachfront resorts are sprinkled along the coast, offering stunning views and direct access to the sandy shores. Imagine waking up to the sound of waves and stepping right onto the beach it's the stuff vacation dreams are made of.

If you're more of a boutique soul, Lanzarote's got chic hotels that scream Instagram-worthy. Trendy designs, comfy beds, and maybe a rooftop pool because, why not? It's your vacation, after all. Your stay becomes not just a necessity but a part of the adventure.

Now, let's talk about the practicalities. Booking in advance is your golden ticket to accommodation success. Lanzarote is a hot destination, and you wouldn't want to miss out on your dream spot because someone beat you to it. Luckily, the internet is your best friend here. A few clicks, and you're all set to secure your home on the island.

But what if you're more of an explorer? Lanzarote's got plenty of charming guesthouses tucked away in its corners. These gems give you a taste of local hospitality and might just become the highlight of your trip. It's like staying with friends – minus the awkward small talk.

For those who prefer a more budget-friendly approach, fear not. Lanzarote's got a solid lineup of apartments and vacation rentals. It's not just about saving a few bucks – it's about having your own space, your own kitchen (if you feel like whipping up a snack), and the freedom to do things your way.

Now, let's address the elephant in the room – Lanzarote's popularity means accommodations fill up fast, especially during peak seasons. So, plan ahead, lock in your dates, and thank yourself later when you're sipping a drink on your private balcony with an ocean view.

But hey, the adventure doesn't stop at your doorstep. Lanzarote's accommodations are strategically placed, giving you easy access to the island's treasures. Whether you're into sunbathing, hiking, or exploring local markets, your temporary abode is the perfect launchpad for your daily escapades.

In the end, your stay in Lanzarote is more than just a place to sleep – it's an integral part of your journey. So, go ahead, pick the accommodation that suits your style, book your spot, and get ready to make yourself at home in this slice of paradise. Your Lanzarote adventure starts the moment you step through the door of your chosen haven, and trust us, it's going to be legendary.

What to Wear

Dressing for Every Adventure

Hey fellow adventurers! Ready to rock your style in Lanzarote? Let's talk threads and get you prepped for every epic moment on this Canary Island paradise.

First up, it's all about the sun. Lanzarote's rays are no joke, so pack those shades and slather on the SPF. A cool hat is not just a fashion statement it's your best defense against the sizzling sun. Think chic and practical – you'll thank yourself later.

Now, let's dive into swimwear. Whether you're hitting up Playa Papagayo or catching waves at Famara Beach, you need a killer swimsuit. Bright colors, bold patterns go wild! This is your chance to flaunt your style against the backdrop of Lanzarote's stunning coastline.

For daytime explorations, comfy kicks are a must. Think sneakers for hikes through Timanfaya National Park or strolling around the vibrant markets in Arrecife. Trust me, blistered feet are not the kind of souvenir you want.

Ladies, throw in a breezy sundress or two. They're perfect for the laid-back island vibes and transition seamlessly from beach to bar. Guys, shorts and a light button-down shirt are your go-to combo for staying cool while looking cool.

Now, let's not forget the evenings. Lanzarote's nightlife is as diverse as its landscapes. A stylish yet casual outfit is your ticket to blending in at the local hotspots. Ladies, a flowy jumpsuit or a cute skirt paired with a tank top is a winner. Gents, opt for smart-casual – think chinos and a crisp polo shirt.

Don't leave your sense of adventure at home – pack it in your day bag! If you're planning to explore volcanic wonders, rugged terrains, or maybe even take a dip in a hidden lagoon, sturdy footwear is a game-changer. Closed-toe shoes are your allies against rocks and unexpected puddles.

Speaking of bags, a backpack is your sidekick for daily adventures. Throw in your essentials – sunscreen, camera, a water bottle, and maybe a snack or two. You never know when a spontaneous picnic might happen.

And for the cool evenings, a light jacket is your secret weapon. Lanzarote's temperatures can dip a bit, especially as the sun bids adieu. A denim jacket or a stylish windbreaker adds that extra layer of comfort and style.

Remember, Lanzarote is all about embracing the natural beauty around you. Keep it simple, keep it breezy, and most importantly, keep it you. This is your adventure, and your wardrobe should reflect the awesome person you are.

So there you have it – your guide to dressing for every adventure in Lanzarote. Pack smart, pack stylish, and get ready to make a splash in the fashion scene of this Canary Island paradise. Adventure awaits, and so does your killer Lanzarote wardrobe!

What to Pack

Essentials for a Perfect Trip

Hey Travel Enthusiasts! Ready to jet off to the sun-soaked paradise of Lanzarote? Before you toss those

flip-flops into your suitcase, let's talk about the essentials to ensure your trip is nothing short of perfect.

First up, let's tackle the wardrobe. Lanzarote's all about that laid-back island vibe, so think light and breezy. Pack your favorite swimsuits, flowy sundresses, and, of course, sunglasses to shield those peepers from the glorious Canarian sun. Don't forget a comfy pair of walking shoes for exploring those volcanic wonders.

Sunscreen is your best friend here. With the sun shining like it's on a mission, it's crucial to protect your skin. Slather on that SPF and enjoy the beaches without the worry of looking like a lobster by day's end.

Now, let's talk tech. While you're there to unplug, a camera is a must-have. Lanzarote is a visual feast – from golden beaches to lunar landscapes – and you'll want to capture it all. Ensure your camera is charged and ready for action.

Speaking of action, water activities are a big deal here. Snorkeling gear, anyone? Dive into the crystal-clear waters and discover the vibrant underwater world. It's like having your own personal National Geographic moment.

Don't forget the power essentials. Adapters are your ticket to keeping your gadgets juiced up. Lanzarote might be a world away, but your devices don't need to feel it.

Now, let's dive into the practical stuff. Your travel documents – the unsung heroes of any trip. Passport? Check. Boarding pass? Check. Travel insurance? Triple check. It might sound like a no-brainer, but you'd be surprised how many forget the golden trio.

Cash is king, even in paradise. While cards are widely accepted, having a bit of local currency on hand can save you from the ATM hunt. Small bills are your best bet – perfect for those charming street markets.

And let's not overlook a reusable water bottle. Staying hydrated is key, especially in that warm Canarian sun.

Fill up before you head out, and you'll be ready for whatever adventures come your way.

Lastly, a good read for those lazy beach days. Grab that novel you've been meaning to devour and let the sound of the waves provide the perfect background music.

Now that your packing list is sorted, get ready for the adventure of a lifetime in Lanzarote. Whether you're into beach bumming, exploring volcanic landscapes, or savoring local cuisine, this Canary Island has it all. So, toss those essentials into your suitcase, and get ready for a trip you'll be reminiscing about for years to come. Lanzarote, here you come! 🌴✈️

Beaches

Sandy Havens and Turquoise Dreams

Welcome to the sun-kissed shores of Lanzarote, where

sandy havens and turquoise dreams come to life. If you're a beach bum at heart, this Canary Island paradise is your ticket to coastal bliss.

Let's start with Playa Blanca, a beach that's as picturesque as it sounds. Soft, golden sands stretch as far as the eye can see, inviting you to kick off your shoes and let the grains tickle your toes. The gentle lull of the waves and the warmth of the sun create a perfect recipe for relaxation.

Famara Beach is a haven for surf enthusiasts and those who appreciate a bit of rugged charm. The wild waves here are a surfer's delight, and the dramatic cliffs that frame the beach add a touch of untamed beauty. Whether you're riding the waves or simply soaking in the view, Famara Beach is a must-visit for beachgoers with a sense of adventure.

For a taste of local life, head to Playa Quemada. This quaint fishing village offers a more laid-back beach experience. Picture colorful fishing boats bobbing in the water, friendly locals, and the scent of fresh seafood wafting through the air. It's a charming escape from the hustle and bustle.

Now, let's talk about Papagayo Beach – a gem that feels like it's been plucked from a postcard. Nestled (oops, there's that word!) on the southern tip of the island, Papagayo is a collection of pristine coves with crystal-clear waters. The vibrant hues of the sea against the backdrop of volcanic cliffs create a visual masterpiece. Snorkelers, this one's for you – the underwater world here is a kaleidoscope of marine life waiting to be discovered.

Moving on to Playa de los Charcos, where tranquility meets untouched beauty. This hidden gem is off the beaten path, offering a sense of seclusion that beach enthusiasts crave. The turquoise waters and the absence of crowds make it a perfect spot to unwind with a good book or simply bask in the serenity.

As you explore Lanzarote's beaches, don't forget the essentials. Slather on that sunscreen, pack your shades, and maybe throw in a floppy hat for good measure. The Canary Island sun is not messing around.

When hunger strikes, you're in for a treat. Beachside chiringuitos (that's Spanish for beach bars) offer a taste of local flavors. From grilled seafood to refreshing cocktails, these spots are a pitstop for indulgence with a view.

Now, for the practical side of things – Lanzarote's beaches are easily accessible, with ample parking and facilities. Whether you're renting a car or hopping on a local bus, reaching these sandy havens is a breeze.

In a nutshell, Lanzarote's beaches are not just destinations they're experiences etched in sun-soaked memories. So, grab your flip-flops, throw on that swimsuit, and get ready to dive into sandy havens and turquoise dreams. Lanzarote awaits, and your beach adventure begins now.

Exploring Papagayo and Famara

Welcome to beach bliss in Lanzarote – where the sun, sand, and surf come together for the ultimate coastal adventure. Get ready to dip your toes in the warm waters of Papagayo and feel the energy of Famara – two beach havens that define the beauty of this Canary Island.

Let's kick things off with Papagayo. This isn't your average beach – it's a slice of paradise. Imagine golden sands meeting crystal-clear waters, with a backdrop of rugged cliffs and swaying palm trees. Papagayo is a postcard-worthy spot, perfect for lazy sunbathing or adventurous water activities.

As you step onto Papagayo's shores, you'll be greeted by a sense of tranquility. The gentle lapping of the waves and the soft caress of the sea breeze create a serene atmosphere that's perfect for unwinding. Find your spot on the beach, lay out your towel, and let the sun work its magic.

But Papagayo isn't just about lounging – it's a haven for water enthusiasts. Snorkeling and swimming are a must, thanks to the clear waters teeming with marine life. Grab a mask, dive in, and discover a vibrant underwater world that rivals any aquarium.

Now, let's talk about Famara. This beach is the epitome of laid-back cool. Stretching for miles along the northwest coast, Famara's vast expanse of sandy goodness is a surfer's paradise. The consistent waves make it an ideal spot for both beginners and seasoned surfers looking to ride the Atlantic swell.

Famara isn't just about the surf – it's a visual spectacle. The towering cliffs that frame the beach create a dramatic backdrop that adds to the overall allure. It's the kind of place where you can take a leisurely stroll, breathe in the salty air, and feel the stress melt away.

When hunger strikes, both Papagayo and Famara have you covered. Local beachside eateries serve up fresh seafood and Canarian delights that will satisfy your taste buds. Picture yourself savoring grilled fish with your toes in the sand – it's a dining experience like no other.

As you explore these beaches, keep an eye out for the unique rock formations that dot the coastline. Nature has sculpted these artistic wonders, creating Instagram-worthy spots that are sure to impress your followers. Don't forget to capture the moment as the sun dips below the horizon, painting the sky in hues of orange and pink.

Whether you're seeking serenity at Papagayo or catching waves at Famara, Lanzarote's beaches offer a diverse range of experiences. And the best part? You don't need a passport to paradise – just a willingness to embrace the laid-back charm of these coastal gems.

So, pack your sunscreen, grab your beach towel, and get ready for a beach day like no other. Papagayo and Famara await, promising sun-soaked memories and a taste of the good life by the sea. Let the beach adventure begin!

Things to Do

Sun, Sand, and Volcanic Wonders

Welcome to the sun-soaked paradise of Lanzarote –
where every day feels like a vacation! If you're

wondering how to make
the most of your time
on this incredible
island, look no further.
Let's dive into the
must-do activities that
will have you falling
head over heels for
Lanzarote.

First up, let's talk beaches. Lanzarote boasts some of the
most stunning stretches of sand you'll ever lay eyes on.
From the laid-back vibes of Playa Blanca to the surfer's
haven at Famara Beach, there's a sandy spot for every
type of beachgoer. Grab your sunscreen, a good book,
and let the sound of the waves be your soundtrack to
relaxation.

Now, let's shift gears to the island's natural wonders.
Timanfaya National Park is a jaw-dropping showcase of
Lanzarote's volcanic prowess. Picture this – lunar-like

landscapes, craters, and lava fields as far as the eye can see. Take a guided tour or venture out on your own – either way, it's a surreal experience you won't soon forget.

Feeling a bit more adventurous? How about a journey into the depths of Cueva de los Verdes? This underground marvel is like nature's own art gallery, with stunning rock formations and a subterranean world waiting to be explored. It's a cool escape from the sun and a chance to marvel at Mother Nature's handiwork.

But Lanzarote isn't just about nature – it's got a vibrant culture that's worth exploring. Head to the island's capital, Arrecife, and stroll through the lively streets. You'll find local markets, charming cafes, and a laid-back atmosphere that perfectly embodies the spirit of Lanzarote. Don't forget to try some local Canarian cuisine while you're at it – your taste buds will thank you.

For a dose of history, a visit to Castillo de San Jose is a must. This fortress-turned-art-gallery offers a glimpse into Lanzarote's past while showcasing contemporary works of art. It's a unique blend of old and new that adds an extra layer to your island experience.

Now, let's talk about exploring the island in style. Rent a bike and pedal your way through the scenic trails of Lanzarote. With the cool breeze in your hair and the sun on your face, it's a fantastic way to see the sights at your own pace. Plus, it's an eco-friendly way to enjoy the island's beauty.

As the day winds down, treat yourself to a front-row seat for Lanzarote's famous sunset. Head to a beachside bar, sip on a refreshing drink, and watch as the sky transforms into a canvas of fiery hues. It's the perfect way to wrap up a day filled with sun, sand, and volcanic wonders.

Lanzarote is a playground for those seeking a perfect blend of natural beauty, adventure, and relaxation. Whether you're exploring volcanic landscapes, lounging on pristine beaches, or immersing yourself in the local culture, this Canary Island gem has something for everyone. So, pack your sense of adventure and get ready to make memories that will last a lifetime in sun-soaked Lanzarote!

Timanfaya National Park Adventure

Welcome to the wild, volcanic wonderland that is Timanfaya National Park in Lanzarote! Get ready for an adventure that'll leave you breathless and craving more. Here's your guide to the must-do activities in this unique slice of nature.

Let's kick things off with the Fire Mountains – the heart and soul of Timanfaya. Picture yourself standing on the edge of craters, surrounded by dramatic landscapes forged by ancient volcanic eruptions. The view alone is enough to make your jaw drop. Don't forget your camera this is Instagram gold!

Next up, hop on a camel safari. Yes, you read that right – camels in Lanzarote! Saddle up and let these gentle giants take you on a ride through the rugged terrain. It's a one-of-a-kind experience that adds a touch of the exotic to your adventure. Plus, the camels make for great photo buddies.

Feeling a bit adventurous? Take a stroll through the Devil's Kitchen. The ground beneath you is literally hot, thanks to the dormant volcanic activity beneath the surface. You'll feel the heat, see steam rising from the ground – it's like walking on another planet. Just remember to wear comfy shoes and stay on the designated paths.

For those who crave a bit of drama, catch the geothermal demonstrations. Watch in awe as park rangers showcase the intense heat beneath the Earth's surface by setting dry grass ablaze with a burst of flames shooting into the air. It's a jaw-dropping display that adds an educational twist to your visit.

Now, let's talk dining – because even in a volcanic landscape, you've got to eat! Head to the El Diablo restaurant, where your meal is cooked using geothermal heat from the ground. It's not every day you get to enjoy a meal prepared by Mother Nature herself. The views from the restaurant aren't too shabby either.

If you're up for a scenic drive, take the Route of the Volcanoes. This winding road offers panoramic views of the park, showcasing the raw beauty of Lanzarote's volcanic terrain. Roll down the windows, feel the breeze, and let the awe-inspiring landscapes unfold before your eyes.

Before you wrap up your Timanfaya adventure, swing by the Visitors' Center. Learn about the geological history of the park through interactive exhibits and gain a deeper appreciation for the forces that shaped this natural wonder.

As you plan your Timanfaya National Park escapade, keep in mind that this is more than a tourist attraction – it's an immersion into the raw, untamed beauty of nature.

So, grab your sun hat, pack some sunscreen, and get ready for a volcanic adventure like no other. Timanfaya is waiting, and it's about to redefine your idea of a thrilling day out. Get ready to explore, discover, and marvel at the extraordinary wonders of Lanzarote's Timanfaya National Park!

Jameos del Agua: A Subterranean Wonderland

Step into a world like no other – the mesmerizing Jameos del Agua in Lanzarote. If you're seeking a unique adventure, this subterranean wonderland is a must-visit on your Lanzarote checklist.

First things first, picture this: underground caves transformed into a magical space that will leave you in awe. Jameos del Agua is a testament to nature's artistry, a place where you'll find surprises at every turn.

Your journey into this underground marvel begins with a stroll through illuminated tunnels. The play of light and shadow creates an enchanting atmosphere, setting the stage for what lies ahead. As you navigate the passages, you'll soon discover a subterranean lake – a hidden gem that adds to the allure of Jameos del Agua.

But it doesn't stop there. The Jameos del Agua complex is a cultural and recreational hub, seamlessly integrated into the volcanic landscape. As you explore further, you'll encounter an open-air auditorium that hosts events and performances. Imagine enjoying live music or a captivating show surrounded by the unique architecture of the caves.

Feeling a bit peckish? Head to the Jameos del Agua restaurant, where you can savor local cuisine in a setting that's nothing short of extraordinary. The combination of good food and the natural surroundings creates a dining experience that's as memorable as it is delicious.

One of the highlights of Jameos del Agua is the crystalline pool. Dive in for a refreshing swim or simply bask in the beauty of this unique setting. The pool area is a tranquil oasis, offering a moment of serenity amidst the subterranean excitement.

As you wander through Jameos del Agua, you'll also come across an underground garden – a green oasis in the heart of the volcanic caves. The careful cultivation of plants adds a touch of nature's vibrancy to the subterranean environment, creating a harmonious blend of the man-made and the natural.

Now, let's talk logistics. Getting to Jameos del Agua is a breeze, and once you're there, the guided tours provide insights into the history and significance of this underground marvel. The site is well-maintained, ensuring a safe and enjoyable experience for visitors of all ages.

Whether you're a solo traveler, a couple seeking a romantic escape, or a family on the lookout for a unique adventure, Jameos del Agua caters to all. The accessibility and diverse offerings make it a must-include destination on your Lanzarote itinerary.

In a nutshell, Jameos del Agua is more than a tourist attraction – it's a journey into a subterranean wonderland that will leave an indelible mark on your Lanzarote memories. So, lace up your comfortable shoes, grab your camera, and get ready to explore the extraordinary beauty that lies beneath the surface of this Canary Island gem. Your underground adventure awaits!

Mirador del Rio: A Vista Like No Other

Welcome to the breathtaking world of Mirador del Rio, where the views are as jaw-dropping as the memories you'll make. Nestled high on a cliff in Lanzarote, this is not your average lookout – it's a vista like no other.

As you make your way to Mirador del Rio, get ready for a scenic drive that's worth the trip itself. The winding roads and dramatic landscapes set the stage for the grand reveal that awaits you at the top.

Once you arrive, prepare to be captivated by panoramic views that stretch as far as the eye can see. The Atlantic Ocean unfolds beneath you, and neighboring islands peek through the horizon. It's a picture-perfect moment that'll have you reaching for your camera – trust us, you'll want to capture this.

But Mirador del Rio is more than just a pretty view. Take a stroll around the observation decks, and you'll find yourself surrounded by a sense of serenity. The fresh sea breeze, the sound of distant waves – it's the kind of tranquility that makes you appreciate the simple joys of life.

Feeling peckish? Mirador del Rio has you covered with a café that serves up refreshments with a side of incredible views. Sip your coffee or enjoy a snack while you soak in the beauty that stretches out before you. It's the perfect pitstop for a moment of relaxation.

For those seeking a bit of history, Mirador del Rio has a story to tell. Originally designed by the island's famous artist and architect, Cesar Manrique, it seamlessly blends into the natural surroundings. The design itself is a testament to Manrique's vision of harmonizing art with nature, creating a space that feels both timeless and contemporary.

Now, if you're an early bird, consider catching the sunrise at Mirador del Rio. Trust us, watching the first rays of light kiss the ocean is a magical experience that words can't quite capture. It's a moment that stays with you long after you've left the cliffside.

As you plan your visit, keep in mind that Mirador del Rio is open year-round, offering different atmospheres with each season. Whether you're basking in the summer sun or enjoying the crisp air of winter, the allure of this panoramic paradise remains constant.

In a nutshell, Mirador del Rio is a must-see in Lanzarote. It's not just a viewpoint – it's an escape, a moment of awe, and a chance to connect with the beauty of the Canary Islands. So, pack your sense of wonder, your camera, and get ready for a vista like no other. Mirador del Rio awaits, and the views are calling your name.

Dining

Savoring Lanzarote's Flavors

Forget sun-kissed beaches and volcanic landscapes for a moment (they'll be waiting!). Lanzarote's magic unfolds

on your plate, in a symphony of fresh, unexpected flavors that dance on your tongue and leave you wanting more. Ditch the tourist traps and dive into the heart of local cuisine, where generations-old recipes whisper secrets of the island's soul.

Seafood Sensation: Lanzarote's shores brim with the ocean's bounty. Dive into a fragrant "lapas y papas" – a volcanic rock platter piled high with garlicky grilled barnacles and wrinkly potatoes, kissed by the salty air. Savor the melt-in-your-mouth "vieja con mojo verde," where the delicate white fish bathes in a vibrant parsley and garlic sauce, bursting with herbaceous tang. And for the adventurous, "pulpo frito" – crispy fried octopus tentacles with a fiery kick – will have you coming back for seconds (and maybe thirds).

Beyond the Beach: Lanzarote's volcanic earth nourishes a treasure trove of unique ingredients. Sample the wrinkly, sun-dried "tomates asados," their sweetness intensified by the sun's embrace. Bite into a warm "gofio escaldado," a hearty porridge made from roasted grains and barley, a taste of island history in every spoonful. And don't miss the "papas con mojo," a humble dish of potatoes transformed into a revelation with a fiery red or a cool green mojo sauce, each bite a tangy explosion.

A Taste of Tradition: Lanzarote's culinary tapestry is woven with threads of family recipes passed down through generations. Seek out a "casa vieja," a traditional restaurant hidden in a charming village, where grandmothers rule the kitchen and plates brim with love. Ask for a "puchero," a hearty stew bursting with vegetables, chickpeas, and maybe even the local "conejo" (rabbit) – a testament to the island's resourcefulness.

Sweet Endings: Don't let the meal end without indulging in Lanzarote's sweet whispers. Bite into a "bienmesabe," a layered pudding of honey, almond, and egg yolk, its richness balanced by the island's signature Malvasia wine. Or savor a "rosquete," a ring of fried dough dusted with cinnamon sugar, its delicate crunch the perfect finale to your culinary adventure.

Lanzarote's flavors are more than just meals; they're stories whispered on the wind, secrets shared with every bite. So ditch the guidebooks and follow your nose – the tastiest adventures are often the ones you stumble upon. With every mouthful, you'll discover a Lanzarote that goes beyond the postcards, a Lanzarote that speaks to your soul, one delicious morsel at a time.

Bonus Tip: Lanzarote's vineyards thrive on volcanic soil, producing unique Malvasia wines. Pair your meal with a local glass and let the flavors intertwine in a delightful dance on your palate.

Remember: Respect local customs and be mindful of food allergies when trying new dishes. Ask questions, engage with the locals, and let your taste buds guide you on this unforgettable culinary journey.

Buen provecho!

Seafood Delights and Local Cuisine

Forget fancy tablecloths and Michelin stars. In Lanzarote, the best dining experiences are sand-between-your-toes affairs, where the soundtrack is crashing waves and the aroma of sizzling garlic prawns hangs heavy in the air. This volcanic island, a jewel in the crown of Spain's Canary Islands, isn't just about dramatic landscapes and lunar-like moonscapes. It's a haven for foodies, a place where the freshest seafood dances on your tongue and local delicacies whisper tales of sun-kissed vineyards and fiery eruptions.

Ocean Symphony on a Plate:

Gambas al Ajillo: Dive into sizzling bliss with plump garlic shrimp, bathed in a garlicky olive oil bath. Close your eyes and let the flavors transport you to a fisherman's shack, waves lapping just steps away.

Lapas a la plancha: These Canarian barnacles, grilled to juicy perfection, are a must-try for the adventurous. Squeeze a lemon wedge, savor the briny bite, and feel like a conquistador discovering new culinary frontiers.

Pulpo a la plancha: Octopus so tender it melts in your mouth, charred just enough to add a smoky whisper. Drizzle with mojo verde, a vibrant green sauce with a kick, and watch your taste buds do a pirouette.

Volcanic Feasts from Land and Sea:

Papas Arrugadas: Wrinkled potatoes, boiled in seawater until their skins are like tiny craters, are a local legend. Dip them in mojo rojo, a spicy red sauce, and let the volcanic earth dance with the sea in your mouth.

Sancocho Canario: This hearty stew, a symphony of chickpeas, meat, and vegetables, warms you from the inside out. Imagine a hug in a bowl, infused with the island's soul-satisfying flavors.

Ropa Vieja: Tender shredded beef, slow-cooked in tomatoes, onions, and herbs, bursts with comfort food vibes. This Canarian classic is guaranteed to leave you wanting seconds (and maybe thirds).

Beyond the Plate:

Dining in Lanzarote isn't just about the food, it's about the experience. Picture yourself:

Sunset tapas: Sharing plates piled high with local bites on a beachfront terrace, as the sun paints the sky in fiery hues. Laughter mingles with the clinking of glasses, and the salty breeze whispers secrets of the island.

Vino con vistas: Sipping Malvasía, a local volcanic wine, overlooking vineyards that cling to rugged cliffs. The air hums with the buzz of conversation and the distant rhythm of the ocean.

Finca feasting: Tucked away in a traditional farmhouse, surrounded by fragrant herb gardens, you dig into a home-cooked feast. Every bite speaks of generations past, of sun-drenched tomatoes and laughter shared under starlit skies.

Lanzarote's culinary scene is a vibrant tapestry woven from fresh seafood, volcanic flavors, and a laid-back island vibe. So grab a fork, ditch the fancy tablecloths, and get ready to have your taste buds serenaded by the rhythm of the ocean and the whispers of ancient volcanoes. This is Lanzarote, where every meal is an adventure, and every bite tells a story.

Now, who's hungry?

P.S. Don't forget to check out the local fish markets, bursting with the day's catch, and charming village bodegas, where friendly faces pour glasses of locally-made wine. In Lanzarote, the best dining experiences are often hidden in plain sight, waiting to be discovered with an open heart and an empty stomach.

Transport

Navigating Like a Local

Lanzarote Wheels: From Cruising Dunes to Sipping Sangria (without getting lost!)

Forget "finding your way" and get ready to conquer Lanzarote like a seasoned island hopper! This ain't your  average transport guide, we're ditching the tourist traps and giving you the lowdown on getting around this volcanic gem like a local. Buckle up, amigos, because Lanzarote's about to become your playground!

Ridin' the Lava Waves: Car Rentals

Lanzarote's not huge, but trust me, you'll wanna explore every nook and cranny. Renting a car is like grabbing the island's remote control – zoom to Timanfaya's fire mountains, blast down to Papagayo's hidden coves, or just cruise the coastal roads with the wind in your hair. It's freedom on four wheels, baby! Just remember, manual transmissions reign supreme here, so brush up on your stick shift if needed.

Buses that Rock (Yeah, Seriously)

Don't write off the Lanzarote bus network just yet! These colorful chariots crisscross the island like clockwork, connecting all the major towns and tourist hotspots. Think vibrant buses, friendly drivers, and views that'll make your Instagram explode. Plus, it's budget-friendly, leaving you more euros for sangria and souvenirs. Download the "Intercity Buses Lanzarote" app for live bus tracking and avoid the "bus stop blues."

Two Wheels, Endless Adventures: Biking in Paradise

Lanzarote's flat terrain and sunshine-soaked roads were practically made for cycling. Picture this: pedaling past vineyards, weaving through charming villages, and stopping for a dip in turquoise waters – all with the ocean breeze whispering in your ears. Rent a bike, join a guided tour, or even grab a tandem for a romantic (and hilarious) adventure. Trust me, two wheels and a volcano view are a match made in island heaven.

Taxis: Your Speedy Shortcut

Need a quick dash to the airport or a spontaneous sunset chase? Taxis are your Lanzarote BFFs. Flag one down, hop in, and let the friendly drivers whisk you away.

They're not the cheapest option, but for short trips or late-night emergencies, they're a lifesaver. Just remember, hailing skills might come in handy, so brush up on your basic Spanish if you can.

Bonus Round: Walking & Hitchhiking (for the Brave Souls)

Lanzarote's small towns and coastal paths are begging to be explored on foot. Lace up your shoes, grab a hat, and soak in the volcanic landscapes, charming architecture, and hidden coves. For the truly adventurous, hitchhiking (autoestop) is a local tradition, but remember, do it at your own risk and only in designated areas.

So, there you have it, Lanzarote transportation decoded! Whether you're a car-loving explorer, a budget-savvy bus hopper, or a cycling enthusiast, this island has a way to get you where you need to go. Just remember, the best journeys are often the unexpected ones, so keep your eyes peeled for hidden gems and let the Lanzarote vibes guide you. Happy exploring!

P.S. Don't forget your sunscreen, a reusable water bottle, and a sense of adventure! Lanzarote's waiting for you…

Renting a Car vs. Public Transport

So, you've landed on Lanzarote, a volcanic playground where lunar landscapes meet crystal-clear coves. Now, the burning question: conquer the island in your own four wheels or hop aboard the local buses? Worry not, fellow adventurer, for I'm here to navigate the pros and cons of each option, helping you choose the ride that'll make your Lanzarote epic.

Renting a Car:

Freedom Fighter: Buckle up for ultimate independence! A car is your trusty steed, whisking you to hidden beaches, quirky villages, and volcanic wonders at your own pace. Want to catch sunrise at Mirador del Rio? No bus schedule holding you back! Craving a spontaneous detour to a roadside winery? Go for it!

Time Traveler: Ditch the rigid bus timetables and explore at your own rhythm. Sleep in for that extra hour, linger longer at Timanfaya National Park, or chase sunset cocktails without worrying about catching the last bus. Lanzarote on your terms, baby!

Space Cadet: Luggage woes? Who needs 'em! Load up your chariot with beach gear, picnic baskets, and souvenirs without fighting for overhead space. Plus, no more lugging those swimsuits back from the beach on a sweltering bus.

But Hold Your Horses:

Parking Palooza: Finding a spot during peak season can be a mini-mission. Be prepared for some creative maneuvers (and maybe a few circles around the block).

Green Thumb Blues: Scooting around in your own car might not be the eco-friendliest choice. Consider eco-conscious car rentals or offset your carbon footprint with some tree-planting goodness.

Budget Bouncer: Renting a car can add a chunk to your Lanzarote budget. Factor in fuel, insurance, and parking fees to get the full picture.

Public Transport:

Social Butterfly: Buses are a great way to mingle with locals and fellow travelers. Strike up conversations, swap island tips, and maybe even score some hidden gem recommendations. Bonus points for brushing up on your Spanish!

Budget Buddy: Public transport is the wallet-friendly champion. Save those euros for volcanic massages, delectable tapas, and sunset catamaran cruises.

Stress-Free Flyer: No navigating roundabouts or deciphering parking signs. Hop on, relax, and watch the volcanic landscapes roll by. Lanzarote on autopilot, here we come!

But Don't Get Too Comfy:

Clock Crusader: Buses follow timetables, sometimes with long gaps between journeys. Be prepared for some waiting and adjusting your itinerary to fit the schedule.

Route Roulette: Not all corners of Lanzarote are as well-connected as others. Some hidden gems might require a longer walk or a taxi ride from the nearest bus stop.

Luggage Limbo: Traveling light is your friend when taking the bus. Ditch the oversized suitcase and pack efficiently to avoid becoming that Tetris-playing passenger blocking the aisle.

So, Who's the Winner?

The Lanzarote champion's belt depends on your travel style! Freedom and flexibility seekers, grab the car keys. Budget-conscious social butterflies, hop on the bus. Ultimately, the perfect ride is the one that takes you on an unforgettable Lanzarote adventure.

Bonus Tip: Combine the two! Rent a car for a few days of exploring hidden coves and volcanic wonders, then switch to public transport for a budget-friendly, social experience in the main towns.

No matter what you choose, Lanzarote awaits with open arms (and volcanic craters). Buckle up, hop on, and get ready to write your own epic Lanzarote story!

Local Culture

Immersing in Lanzarote's Heritage

Step into the vibrant tapestry of Lanzarote's local culture, where every corner tells a story and every moment is a

celebration of authenticity. This Canary Island gem is not just about breathtaking landscapes; it's a journey into the heart and soul of a community rich in tradition and charm.

Begin your cultural exploration in the lively streets of Arrecife, the island's capital. Here, you'll find a perfect blend of old-world charm and modern vibrancy. Take a leisurely stroll through the bustling markets, where local artisans showcase their crafts, and the aroma of freshly brewed coffee fills the air.

As you wander, you'll notice the unique architecture that reflects Lanzarote's history. Whitewashed buildings with green and blue accents create a picturesque scene against the azure sky. It's a visual feast that transports you to a time where simplicity and elegance were the hallmarks of daily life.

Don't miss the chance to indulge in the local gastronomic delights. Lanzarote's cuisine is a testament to its cultural diversity and connection to the land. From savory tapas to mouthwatering seafood dishes, each bite is a savory journey through the island's culinary heritage.

Venture beyond the tourist hotspots to discover hidden gems where locals gather. Strike up a conversation with the friendly residents, and you'll find a warmth and hospitality that defines the spirit of Lanzarote. They'll gladly share tales of the island's history, customs, and the significance of their traditions.

For a deeper dive into Lanzarote's past, make your way to the island's museums. The Museum of International and Contemporary Art (MIAC) in Arrecife is a treasure trove of artistic expression, showcasing works that reflect the island's cultural evolution. It's a visual odyssey that sheds light on Lanzarote's artistic soul.

As you explore the island, keep an eye out for local events and festivals. These lively gatherings offer a firsthand experience of Lanzarote's traditions. From vibrant carnivals to folkloric celebrations, you'll find yourself dancing to the rhythms of local music and savoring the joyous atmosphere.

To truly connect with Lanzarote's heritage, consider attending a traditional Canarian dance performance. The rhythmic beats and colorful costumes will transport you to a world where each movement tells a story of the island's history and resilience.

In your cultural odyssey, don't forget to appreciate the indigenous crafts of Lanzarote. Local markets showcase handmade pottery, intricate lacework, and unique jewelry, each piece reflecting the skill and passion of the artisans who call the island home.

In essence, immersing yourself in Lanzarote's heritage is not just an exploration; it's a celebration of a living, breathing culture that welcomes visitors with open arms. So, as you venture beyond the beaches and delve into the heart of the island, be prepared to be enchanted by the stories, flavors, and traditions that make Lanzarote a cultural haven waiting to be discovered.

Exploring César Manrique's Artistic Legacy

Welcome to a journey through the artistic wonders of César Manrique, a true visionary whose influence has left an indelible mark on the cultural landscape of

Lanzarote. Prepare to be captivated as we unravel the vibrant tapestry of his artistic legacy.

César Manrique, a native son of Lanzarote, seamlessly blended his love for art, architecture, and the natural beauty of the island. His creations are not just landmarks but living, breathing testaments to the harmonious relationship between human ingenuity and the environment.

Start your exploration at the Jameos del Agua, a mesmerizing creation born from a volcanic tunnel. Here, Manrique transformed a natural formation into a cultural space where art and nature coexist. Picture yourself strolling through subterranean chambers adorned with his sculptures, a surreal experience that brings together the ancient and the avant-garde.

Next on the itinerary is the Mirador del Río, a breathtaking lookout point perched atop the cliffs of Famara. Manrique's touch is evident in the seamless integration of the building into the surroundings. As you gaze upon the panoramic views, you'll appreciate his mastery in framing nature as a living canvas.

Manrique's artistic influence extends to the heart of Lanzarote – the capital city, Arrecife. Visit the Castillo de San José, a fortress turned contemporary art museum designed by Manrique himself. The juxtaposition of modern art against historic walls creates a dynamic space that reflects the island's ever-evolving cultural identity.

For a taste of local flavor, venture into Teguise, where the Fundación César Manrique resides. This foundation, housed in Manrique's former residence, pays homage to the artist's life and works. It's a treasure trove of his paintings, sculptures, and personal artifacts, offering an intimate glimpse into the mind of a creative genius.

Now, let's talk about the iconic wind sculptures that dot the landscape of Lanzarote. Manrique's wind toys, locally known as "Juguetes del Viento," are playful installations that dance with the breeze. From roundabouts to public spaces, these whimsical creations add a touch of enchantment to the island's streets.

As you explore César Manrique's artistic legacy, you'll notice a common thread – a deep reverence for Lanzarote's natural beauty. His creations serve as a reminder that art doesn't have to compete with nature; it can complement and enhance it.

Diving into César Manrique's artistic legacy is not just a cultural excursion; it's a journey into the soul of Lanzarote. Each creation tells a story of a man deeply connected to his roots, a man who envisioned a harmonious coexistence between art and the environment. So, put on your explorer hat, open your eyes to the wonders around you, and let César Manrique's artistic legacy be your guide to the heart of Lanzarote's local culture.

Safety Tips

Ensuring Well-being in Paradise

Ah, paradise – the dreamy escape we all crave. Whether you're jetting off to a tropical island or exploring a hidden gem, safety should always be your travel companion. Let's talk about how to keep that vacation glow without compromising on well-being.

First things first, let's tackle the sun. Yes, we all love a good tan, but let's not get crispy. Slather on that sunscreen like it's your secret weapon against sunburn. Go for SPF 30 or higher, and don't forget those often overlooked spots – ears, feet, and the back of your neck. Trust me; your skin will thank you later.

Staying hydrated is not just a suggestion; it's a survival tactic. Paradise might be all about sipping coconut water by the beach, but throw in a water bottle to the mix. Keep it filled, and take regular sips. It's the easiest way to beat the heat and ensure you're ready for all those island adventures.

Now, let's talk about the sea – as mesmerizing as it is, respect the ocean. Even if you're a pro swimmer, always be mindful of the currents. If the waves are giving off a "Baywatch" vibe, maybe it's not the best time for a dip. Safety first, fun second.

Footwear matters, even in paradise. Flip-flops are cute, but consider investing in some sturdy sandals for those impromptu hikes or walks on uneven terrain. Your feet will thank you, and you won't miss out on any of the breathtaking views.

Speaking of hikes, let someone know your whereabouts. Whether you're conquering a mountain or just strolling through a quaint town, it's always good to have a buddy system, even if your buddy is back at the hotel. Share your plans, and make sure your phone is charged – it's your lifeline to the outside world.

Let's address the infamous traveler's tummy. Paradise is not the place to experiment with street food without caution. Enjoy the local cuisine, but do so with a bit of discretion. Stick to bottled water, avoid ice in your drinks, and maybe save the daring food adventures for when you're back home.

If you're venturing into the nightlife scene, keep your wits about you. Yes, it's tempting to let loose, but moderation is key. Have a blast, but be aware of your surroundings. Traveling is about creating memories, not blackouts.

Last but certainly not least, secure your belongings. Paradise might feel like a bubble of bliss, but petty theft is a universal language. Keep your valuables close, be mindful of your surroundings, and consider investing in a small lock for your luggage. It's the little things that can make a big difference.

So, there you have it – your guide to ensuring well-being in paradise. Because a vacation is all about relaxation and enjoyment, and these safety tips are your passport to worry-free bliss. Now, go forth and conquer that paradise with the wisdom of a seasoned traveler. Your well-being deserves it!

Weather Precautions and Outdoor Safety

Hey there, adventure seekers! Planning a trip to the sun-soaked paradise of Lanzarote? Before you dive headfirst into the excitement, let's talk safety. We're all about making sure your island getaway is not just fun but safe too. So, buckle up for some weather precautions and outdoor safety tips that will keep you smiling from ear to ear.

First things first, let's chat about the weather. Lanzarote is known for its glorious sunshine, but the sun here means serious business. Slather on that sunscreen like it's your job, especially if you plan on basking in the beach vibes. A hat and sunglasses are not just accessories – they're your best buddies in the fight against the sun's rays.

Hydration is key, folks! With the sun shining high and mighty, it's easy to get caught up in the moment and forget to sip some H_2O. Keep a water bottle handy, and trust us, your body will thank you for it. Dehydration is not the souvenir you want to bring back from your vacation.

Now, let's talk about the wind. Lanzarote can be a bit of a windy wonderland, especially in certain areas. If you're planning on hitting the waves for some water sports, double-check those wind conditions. It's all about having a blast, not getting blown away!

If you're venturing into the wild side of Lanzarote's landscapes, sturdy footwear is your go-to gear. Whether you're hiking volcanic trails or strolling through rocky terrains, protect those feet. Comfort and safety – the dynamic duo of outdoor exploration.

Swimming enthusiasts, listen up! While Lanzarote's beaches are a dream, the ocean currents can be a bit cheeky. Always be aware of the water conditions and, if needed, stick to the designated swimming areas. Safety first, and then the splashy fun can commence.

Now, let's talk about the nightlife. Lanzarote knows how to throw a party, but a night out doesn't mean throwing caution to the wind. Keep an eye on your belongings, stay in well-lit areas, and, of course, enjoy responsibly. No one wants a legendary vacation story that starts with, "Remember that time I got lost?"

In case of any emergencies because it's always better to be safe than sorry familiarize yourself with the local emergency numbers and the location of the nearest medical facilities. It's like having a superhero's hotline on speed dial.

Lastly, when it comes to your island adventures, always trust your instincts. If something doesn't feel right, it probably isn't. Whether you're exploring the natural wonders or the local hotspots, your safety is the top priority.

So, there you have it your guide to weather precautions and outdoor safety in Lanzarote. Now, armed with these tips, go out there and make some unforgettable memories. The island is waiting, and so is the adventure of a lifetime. Stay safe, stay awesome, and soak in all the wonders Lanzarote has to offer!

Lanzarote After Dark

Nightlife Adventures Await

Get ready to light up your nights in Lanzarote! When the sun sets, the island transforms into a vibrant playground  of nightlife delights. Whether you're into laid-back lounges, pumping clubs, or beachside bars, Lanzarote has the after-dark scene to match your every mood.

For those seeking a more relaxed vibe, start your evening at one of the beachfront bars. Picture this: toes in the sand, a cool drink in hand, and the sound of waves providing the soundtrack to your night. From lively Playa Blanca to the trendy spots in Puerto del Carmen, these beach bars are the perfect kickoff to your nightlife adventures.

If you're in the mood to dance the night away, Puerto del Carmen is your go-to destination. The strip comes alive after dark with a kaleidoscope of lights, music pumping from every corner, and an infectious energy that's hard to resist. Dive into the beats at one of the electrifying clubs, and let the rhythm carry you into the early morning hours.

For a taste of the local flavor, head to Arrecife. This capital city knows how to party, offering a mix of traditional Canarian vibes and modern nightlife. Wander through the charming streets, discover hidden gems, and stumble upon lively bars where locals and visitors come together for a night to remember.

Lanzarote's nightlife isn't just about music and cocktails it's also a culinary adventure. Indulge your taste buds in the late-night food scene. From tapas joints to street food vendors, the options are as diverse as the crowd. Imagine savoring local flavors under the stars, surrounded by the buzz of a lively night out.

Looking for a more intimate setting? Explore the island's cozy pubs and lounges. These hidden gems offer a quieter escape, perfect for a laid-back evening with friends or a romantic night out. Sip on expertly crafted cocktails, enjoy live music, and soak in the ambiance that makes each venue unique.

The best part? Lanzarote's nightlife isn't confined to one area it's a journey of discovery across the entire island. Hop from one hotspot to another, and you'll find that each locale has its own charm and character, ensuring your nights are as diverse as your days.

As you dive into Lanzarote's nightlife scene, keep in mind the local customs and flavors. Embrace the Canarian spirit, chat with the friendly locals, and let the night unfold organically. Whether you're a party animal, a laid-back lounger, or somewhere in between, Lanzarote's nightlife adventures await – and they're bound to leave you with unforgettable memories.

So, what are you waiting for? When the sun sets in Lanzarote, the real magic begins. Grab your dancing shoes, rally your crew, and get ready for a night of pure island vibes. Your Lanzarote after-dark adventure is about to begin – and it's going to be epic. Cheers to the nights you'll never forget!

Stargazing in the Dark Sky Reserve

Welcome to the otherworldly charm of Lanzarote after the sun bids farewell! If you're yearning for a celestial spectacle, the Dark Sky Reserve in Lanzarote is your front-row seat to a cosmic show like no other.

As the sun sets, the real magic begins. Lanzarote's Dark Sky Reserve, located away from the city lights, offers an unobstructed view of the night sky. Picture this: a canvas filled with countless stars, constellations telling ancient tales, and the Milky Way painting a shimmering stripe across the heavens.

Grab a blanket, find a comfy spot, and let your gaze wander. The sheer number of stars visible in Lanzarote's night sky is mind-boggling. It's a celestial dance that captivates both seasoned stargazers and those new to the wonders above.

One of the prime locations for this celestial extravaganza is the Mirador del Rio. Perched on a clifftop, it not only provides a stunning view of the island but also serves as an ideal spot for stargazing. Imagine the cool night breeze on your face as you lose yourself in the vastness of the universe.

But the Dark Sky Reserve isn't just about stars. The reserve hosts regular astronomy events, where expert astronomers guide you through the intricacies of the night sky. Telescopes are set up, revealing planets, distant galaxies, and celestial phenomena that seem almost surreal.

What makes Lanzarote's Dark Sky Reserve truly special is the commitment to preserving the natural darkness. The island has implemented measures to minimize light pollution, ensuring an unparalleled stargazing experience. It's like having a front-row seat to the universe's grand performance.

For those wanting to take their stargazing to the next level, consider joining a guided night tour. Local astronomers share their knowledge, pointing out celestial wonders and unraveling the mysteries of the cosmos. It's an educational and awe-inspiring journey into the depths of space.

Lanzarote's night sky isn't just for astronomy enthusiasts – it's for anyone who appreciates the beauty of a star-studded night. Couples looking for a romantic evening, families seeking a unique adventure, or solo travelers in search of a moment of cosmic connection – the Dark Sky Reserve welcomes all.

Before you head out on your nocturnal escapade, pack some essentials. A cozy jacket, a thermos of hot cocoa, and perhaps a snack to keep you fueled during your celestial exploration. And don't forget your camera – capturing the brilliance of the night sky in Lanzarote is a memory you'll want to hold onto.

So, as the day transforms into night, venture into the enchanting realm of Lanzarote's Dark Sky Reserve. It's not just stargazing; it's an invitation to marvel at the universe's grandeur. Join the cosmic celebration, and let the magic of the night sky in Lanzarote leave you starry-eyed and filled with wonder. Your celestial adventure awaits!

Health

Staying Fit During Your Stay

Welcome to Lanzarote, where the sun shines, the beaches beckon, and staying fit is a breeze. Vacation doesn't mean putting your health on pausein fact, it's the perfect opportunity to embrace wellness in paradise.

Let's start with the obvious the beaches. Lanzarote's coastline isn't just for lazy lounging (though that's totally allowed). Take a stroll along the shore, feel the sand between your toes, and let the waves be your soundtrack. It's a low-key workout with a view that beats any gym.

If you're into a more structured fitness routine, Lanzarote has you covered. Many hotels offer well-equipped fitness centers, so you can squeeze in a workout without missing a beat. Pump some iron, hit the treadmill, and reward yourself with a dip in the pool afterward fitness with a side of relaxation.

Now, let's talk outdoor activities. Lanzarote's terrain is a natural playground for the fitness-minded. Hiking trails crisscross the island, offering a chance to get your heart pumping while surrounded by breathtaking landscapes.

Pack some water, lace up your sneakers, and hit the trails for a dose of nature-infused exercise.

For the water enthusiasts, Lanzarote's beaches aren't just for sunbathing. Take advantage of the crystal-clear waters with some water sports action. Whether it's paddleboarding, surfing, or a friendly game of beach volleyball, there's no shortage of ways to stay active while enjoying the ocean breeze.

Speaking of breezes, how about a cycling adventure? Lanzarote's bike-friendly roads and scenic routes make it a cyclist's dream. Rent a bike, pedal through the picturesque villages, and discover the island on two wheels. It's a fun and eco-friendly way to explore while keeping your fitness goals in check.

Now, let's not forget the local flavors. Lanzarote's culinary scene is a delightful mix of fresh seafood, local produce, and Canarian specialties. While indulging in the deliciousness, keep an eye on portion sizes and balance. It's all about savoring the flavors without overindulging – a mindful approach to eating that complements your active vacation.

And of course, hydration is key. With the sun kissing your skin, it's essential to keep the water flowing. Carry a reusable water bottle, sip throughout the day, and stay refreshed. Your body will thank you, and you'll be ready for whatever adventures Lanzarote throws your way.

Remember, staying fit in Lanzarote isn't about strict regimens or intense workouts. It's about finding joy in movement, embracing the island's natural beauty, and making choices that align with your well-being. Whether you're a fitness fanatic or just looking to keep things in balance, Lanzarote offers the perfect backdrop for a healthy and happy vacation.

So, lace up those sneakers, grab your swimsuit, and get ready to blend fitness with fun in Lanzarote. Your health and happiness are on the itinerary, and this island paradise is the ultimate playground for your well-being.

Healthcare Facilities and Services

Welcome to a healthier you in Lanzarote! Your well-being is our priority, and this captivating island has more to offer than just stunning landscapes. Let's explore the healthcare facilities and services that ensure you stay in tip-top shape during your stay.

First off, Lanzarote boasts modern and well-equipped medical facilities. You'll find hospitals and clinics across the island, ready to provide top-notch care. The healthcare professionals here are not only skilled but also friendly, making your health concerns feel a little less daunting.

In case of minor ailments or health queries, pharmacies are your go-to heroes. They're scattered conveniently, and the pharmacists are knowledgeable and approachable. From sunburn relief to travel essentials, they've got you covered. So, if you forgot to pack your sunscreen, don't worry the local pharmacy is just a short walk away.

For more serious health matters, the island's hospitals are equipped with state-of-the-art facilities. Rest assured, you're in capable hands if the need arises. The healthcare system in Lanzarote is designed to cater to residents and visitors alike, ensuring everyone receives the care they deserve.

Now, let's talk about health and wellness services that go beyond the conventional. Lanzarote offers a range of alternative therapies and wellness centers that focus on holistic well-being. From yoga retreats to spa experiences, you can recharge your mind, body, and soul in this tranquil haven.

The island's commitment to health extends to its culinary scene. Many restaurants feature fresh, local ingredients that contribute to a wholesome dining experience. Enjoy a variety of dishes that not only tantalize your taste buds but also nourish your body.

Staying active is a breeze in Lanzarote. The island's diverse terrain invites you to explore on foot, by bike, or even on the water. Whether it's a leisurely beachfront stroll or an adrenaline-pumping water sports adventure, you'll find plenty of opportunities to keep your body moving.

For those who prioritize fitness, there are gyms and fitness centers across the island. Stay on track with your workout routine while soaking in the scenic views – it's a win-win situation. Many accommodations also offer fitness facilities, so you can break a sweat without venturing too far.

It's worth noting that Lanzarote's commitment to health extends to its commitment to safety. The island follows stringent health and safety protocols, ensuring a clean and secure environment for residents and visitors. You can explore with peace of mind, knowing that your well-being is a top priority.

Lanzarote is not just a feast for the eyes – it's a haven for your health. With a robust healthcare system, wellness services, and a focus on clean living, this island ensures you have everything you need to stay healthy and happy. So, whether you're here for the landscapes, the cuisine, or the wellness experiences, know that your well-being is in good hands in Lanzarote. Cheers to a healthier, happier you!

Emergency

Your Guide to Unexpected Situations

Hey there, intrepid traveler! While we're all about fun in the sun and making memories, it's good to be prepared for the unexpected, right? So, let's talk about being your own hero in case of unexpected situations during your Lanzarote adventure.

First things first emergencies happen, but there's no need to panic. Lanzarote's got you covered with reliable emergency services. Need medical assistance? Dial 112, and help is on the way. The island has well-equipped medical facilities and pharmacies, so you can get back to your vacay vibe ASAP.

Now, let's tackle the not-so-fun topic: lost stuff. It happens to the best of us. If you misplace something valuable or crucial, head to the nearest police station. They're pros at helping you out, whether it's a misplaced passport or a forgotten sun hat. Keep calm, report the situation, and let them work their magic.

Weather can be unpredictable, even in paradise. If you find yourself caught in a sudden rain shower or feeling the heat a bit too much, don't fret. Grab some shade, sip on a cool drink, and let the weather do its thing. It's all part of the adventure, right?

Let's talk about the big one earthquakes. Lanzarote is in a seismic zone, but the good news is that the island is well-prepared. If you feel the ground shake, remember the drill: drop, cover, and hold on. Most buildings are designed to handle seismic activity, so stay calm, follow safety guidelines, and you'll be back to your vacation groove in no time.

Lost your way exploring the volcanic landscapes? No worries it happens to the best explorers. Use landmarks, check your phone map, and don't hesitate to ask a friendly local for directions. They're more than happy to point you in the right direction.

Now, let's talk about those little mishaps we'd rather avoid but sometimes can't. If you find yourself with a minor injury or a pesky sunburn, head to the nearest pharmacy. The pharmacists are superheroes in white coats, ready with advice and remedies to get you back on your feet.

Travel insurance is your trusty sidekick in these situations. It's like a safety net for your adventure, covering unexpected medical expenses or trip disruptions. Before you jet off, make sure you've got your insurance sorted – it's the unsung hero of worry-free travel.

Last but not least, common sense is your best friend. Keep an eye on your belongings, stay hydrated, and be aware of your surroundings. Lanzarote is a friendly paradise, and a little bit of awareness goes a long way in ensuring your trip stays as dreamy as you imagined.

So, there you have it – your guide to handling unexpected situations in Lanzarote. Remember, every bump in the road is just a detour to a new adventure. Stay safe, stay chill, and let the good times roll on this beautiful Canary Island. Your Lanzarote escapade is waiting – unexpected twists and all!

Contacts and Emergency Procedures

Hey there, savvy traveler! We're all about fun in the sun and making memories, but let's talk real talk for a sec – the nitty-gritty of staying safe in Lanzarote. No buzzkill, just good ol' practical tips to keep your adventure smooth.

First off, you gotta have your contacts in order. Save the local emergency numbers – it's 112 for all things urgent.

Whether it's a bag left on a bus or a more serious hiccup, this number is your go-to lifeline.

Now, if you find yourself in a medical pickle, fear not. Lanzarote's got hospitals and clinics that are up to the task. The Arrecife General Hospital is a solid choice, and there are health centers sprinkled around the island. Google Maps is your friend – type in "health center" or "hospital," and you're good to go.

But let's not go down that road if we don't have to. Prevention is the name of the game. Slather on that sunscreen – the Lanzarote sun doesn't mess around. It's your best defense against looking like a lobster after a day at the beach.

Speaking of beaches, keep an eye on those waves. Lanzarote's shores are a water sports paradise, but safety first, my friend. Check the local conditions, pay attention to flags, and if the lifeguard says it's a no-go, listen up.

Now, let's talk about your stuff. Losing your passport or wallet is like a bad dream, but hey, it happens. Keep photocopies of important documents in a separate place – just in case. And while you're at it, snap a pic of your passport and store it in the cloud. It's the 21st century version of a safety net.

Now, onto the language game. English is your trusty sidekick in tourist hotspots, but a little Spanish goes a long way. "Hola" and "gracias" might be basic, but they're like magic words that can turn a frown upside down.

But what if the unexpected happens? Say you miss the last bus or your sense of direction takes a vacation. Cue the GPS on your phone – it's a lifesaver. Download an offline map of Lanzarote before you jet off, and you'll be navigating like a local in no time.

Lastly, let's talk about the unsung hero – travel insurance. Yeah, it's not the sexiest topic, but it's the safety net you'll be grateful for if Murphy's Law decides to pay a visit.

So there you have it, friend. Lanzarote's all about sun, sea, and good vibes, but a dash of common sense goes a long way. Stay safe, have a blast, and make those memories – the right kind of memories, of course. Cheers to your epic Lanzarote adventure! 🌴✈️

Useful Phrases

Connecting with Local Words

Welcome to Lanzarote, where the sun shines, the waves beckon, and the locals welcome you with open arms! As you dive into this Canarian adventure, it's always a plus to sprinkle a bit of local lingo into your conversations. So, let's arm you with some handy phrases to make your stay even more memorable.

1. ¡Hola! (Hello!)
Kick off your conversations with a friendly "¡Hola!" It's the universal greeting that opens doors and brings smiles. Whether you're entering a café, shop, or just passing by someone on the street, a cheerful "¡Hola!" is your go-to icebreaker.

2. Por favor (Please) and Gracias (Thank you)
Manners matter everywhere, and Lanzarote is no exception. Saying "**por favor**" when making a request and "**gracias**" when expressing gratitude will earn you extra points with the locals. It's a small effort that goes a long way.

3. ¿Cuánto cuesta? (How much does it cost?)

Shopping spree on the horizon? Whether you're eyeing a cute souvenir or a fresh batch of local produce at the market, knowing "¿**Cuánto cuesta**?" will help you navigate the world of prices with confidence.

4. La cuenta, por favor (The bill, please)

After a delightful meal at a local eatery, when you're ready to wrap it up, catch the server's attention with "**La cuenta, por favor**." It's the polite way to signal that you're ready to settle the tab.

5. ¿Dónde está…? (Where is…?)

Lost in the charming streets of Lanzarote? Don't hesitate to ask "¿**Dónde está…?**" Whether it's the nearest beach, the bus stop, or that hidden gem of a restaurant, the locals will be more than happy to point you in the right direction.

6. ¡Salud! (Cheers!)

Planning to toast to your Lanzarote adventure? Raise your glass and exclaim, "¡Salud!" It's the perfect way to share a celebratory moment and connect with fellow revelers.

7. ¿Puedo tomar una foto? (Can I take a photo?)

When you stumble upon a view that's too good to be true or you want to capture the essence of a local market, ask politely, "¿Puedo tomar una foto?" It's a courteous way to respect the surroundings and make memories.

8. ¿Hablas inglés? (Do you speak English?)
While many locals in Lanzarote are fluent in English, asking "¿Hablas inglés?" shows your willingness to bridge any language gaps. It's a handy phrase that can come to the rescue when needed.

9. Estoy perdido/a (I'm lost)
If you find yourself off the beaten path and need a little guidance, saying "Estoy perdido/a" will let others know you could use a helping hand. Locals are known for their friendliness, and they'll likely be happy to assist you.

10. ¡Hasta luego! (See you later!)
As your time in Lanzarote winds down, bid farewell with a cheerful "¡Hasta luego!" It's a friendly way to express your hope for future encounters and leaves the door open for return visits.

So, armed with these local phrases, go forth and connect with the vibrant spirit of Lanzarote. Whether you're sipping coffee in a local café or strolling along the coastline, these words will make your journey even richer. ¡Buena suerte! (Good luck!)

Basic Spanish Phrases for Travelers

Hola, fellow traveler! If you're gearing up for a trip to the beautiful island of Lanzarote, knowing a few basic Spanish phrases can make your adventure even more enjoyable. Let's skip the language barriers and dive into some handy expressions that will have you mingling with the locals in no time.

1. Greetings and Polite Expressions:
   - *¡Hola! - Hello!*
   - *Buenos días - Good morning*
   - *Buenas tardes - Good afternoon*
   - *Buenas noches - Good evening/night*
   - *Por favor - Please*
   - *Gracias - Thank you*
   - *De nada - You're welcome*

2. Asking for Help:
   - *¿Hablas inglés? - Do you speak English?*
   - *Necesito ayuda - I need help*
   - *¿Dónde está el baño? - Where is the bathroom?*
   - *¿Puede ayudarme, por favor? - Can you help me, please?*

3. Ordering Food and Drinks:
   - *Quisiera un café, por favor - I would like a coffee, please*

- La cuenta, por favor - The bill, please

- ¿Tienen menú en inglés? - Do you have an English menu?

- Está delicioso - It's delicious

4. Directions and Transportation:

- ¿Cómo llego a la playa? - How do I get to the beach?

- Estoy perdido/a - I am lost

- ¿Cuánto cuesta el billete? - How much is the ticket?

- ¿Dónde está la estación de autobuses? - Where is the bus station?

5. Shopping Essentials:

- ¿Cuánto cuesta esto? - How much does this cost?

- ¿Tienen esta camiseta en otra talla? - Do you have this shirt in another size?

- ¿Aceptan tarjetas de crédito? - Do you accept credit cards?

6. Emergencies:

- ¡Ayuda! - Help!

- Necesito un médico - I need a doctor

- Llame a la policía - Call the police

- Estoy perdiendo el vuelo - I am missing the flight

7. Expressing Gratitude:

- Muchas gracias - Many thanks

- Estoy muy agradecido/a - I am very grateful

- Gracias por su amabilidad - Thank you for your kindness

Mastering these basic Spanish phrases will not only make your time in Lanzarote smoother but also show the locals that you've put in a bit of effort to connect with their culture. So, pack these phrases along with your sunscreen, and get ready for an amazing adventure on this sun-kissed island. ¡Buena suerte! (Good luck!)

Map of Lanzarote

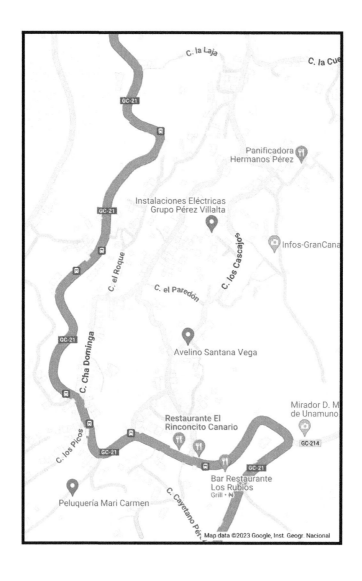

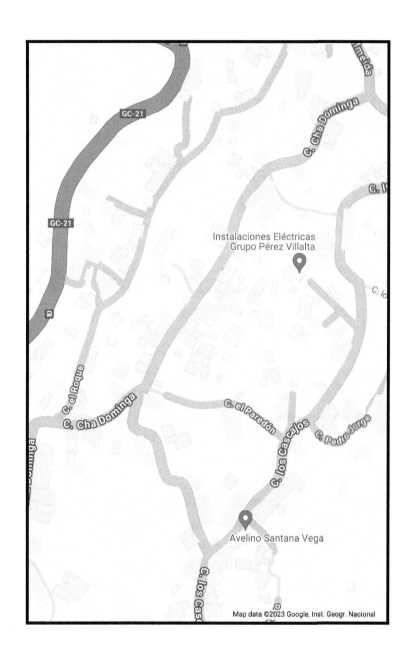

Conclusion

And there you have it, fellow adventurers – the grand finale of your Lanzarote travel escapade! If you've made it this far, congratulations on being the proud owner of the quirkiest, friendliest guidebook this side of the Atlantic.

As you close the last page, take a moment to reflect on the gems you've uncovered. From the sun-drenched beaches that practically beg for a beach towel, to the lunar-like landscapes that left you questioning if you accidentally boarded a rocket to the moon – Lanzarote has surely etched its way into your heart.

But what makes this guidebook the hidden treasure in your collection? Well, besides being your passport to paradise, it's your witty travel companion. We've spared you the generic jargon and opted for a dose of humor to keep those travel vibes light and lively.

Whether you followed our lead to the best local eateries, embraced the art of navigating the roundabouts like a pro, or simply laughed at our attempts to describe the indescribable beauty of Timanfaya National Park, we hope this guide added a splash of fun to your Lanzarote adventure.

And to our dear reader, YOU the unsung hero of this epic journey. Thank you for choosing our guidebook to be your trusty sidekick. We know you have options, but you went with the one that promises info with a side of giggles, and for that, we salute you.

As you embark on your own Lanzarote escapade armed with this guidebook, remember, it's not just a book – it's a backstage pass to the island's best-kept secrets. Use it as your treasure map, your laughter-inducing bedtime story, or even as a makeshift fan during those sizzling afternoons on the beach.

In the spirit of Lanzarote's carefree vibe, we leave you with a parting thought: "Why did the traveler bring a ladder to the beach? Because they wanted to get to the high tide!" Corny, we know, but hey, laughter is the best travel companion, right?

So, go forth, dear reader, and conquer Lanzarote with the knowledge and laughter you've gained from this guidebook. Until our paths cross again in the vast world of travel, stay adventurous, stay curious, and most importantly, stay smiling.

Safe travels and big hugs,
CHERYL JOHN

Printed in Great Britain
by Amazon